THE DOG WITH NINE LIVES

THE DOG WITH NINE LIVES

Della Galton

Published by Accent Press Ltd – 2010

ISBN 9781907726330

Copyright © Della Galton 2010

For Maggie Avgerinou with love and thanks, and every other anonymous dog rescuer working tirelessly out there

Acknowledgements

I would like to thank the following people: all those lovely people on Pefkos beach who helped with the rescue; all at RAWS, especially Maggie Avgerinou; Sandra and Colin Forrest; Dominic Groves; Tony and Adam Millward; Knightwood Quarantine Kennels; All at Walton Lodge Veterinary Group, especially Kate and Jenny.
All at Weatherbury Veterinary Clinic, especially Philippa; Jo and Paul at Tricks4Treats.

CHAPTER ONE

I will not get involved

I COULDN'T REMEMBER THE last time I'd felt so content. The hot sun burned down on my face and beyond my closed eyelids sun patterns danced. I could hear the swish of the sea and the shouts of children playing in the waves, and the scent of burgers from a nearby café wafted on the faint breeze.

This was the life, I thought in my half dozing stupor. After a hectic week in Rhodes where I'd been taking photographs at my sister-in-law, Sandra's, wedding it was lovely to be able to relax for a while. We'd been here four days. It was my first visit to the picturesque island, and I was planning to come again.

Suddenly my idyll was shattered by a cold wet hand dripping sea water on to my arm and an urgent voice in my ear.

'Look, Della, there's a dog.'

'I've seen one before,' I said, still half asleep and determined to stay that way.

'It's a stray dog. It's really cute. Go on, have a look.' Sandra isn't the type to give up easily.

I opened one eye and caught a blurred image of a dog running by in the soft sand.

'Lovely,' I said, because I was obviously expected to say something.

'I thought you liked dogs.' Sandra's voice was disgruntled.

'I do like dogs.'

'What sort do you think it is?'

I opened both eyes now and squinted against the glare. The dog was chocolate brown with floppy ears and a skinny stick of a tail.

'A right mixture – maybe a bit of Labrador. I shouldn't think she's a pedigree!'

My irony was wasted on Sandra, but after that, she left me to my dreams again, and my dreams were of dogs. I wasn't really indifferent to them, far from it. I had three of my own at home, all of them rescue dogs. To be honest, I was more worried that I might get involved and I couldn't afford to care too much about stray dogs in Greece.

Although I admired people who rescued dogs from horrendous lives in other countries, I was strongly of the opinion that if you had that sort of money going spare, it would be better spent in England. How many dogs could be helped for the cost of bringing just one stray into the UK? Shouldn't charity begin at home?

I'd rescued lots of dogs across the years, which was something Sandra knew very well, but there was no way I was getting involved with this one. She seemed quite happy running about on the sand, and scrounging food from holidaymakers.

I watched her for a while. She was pretty smart. She would suss out her target first, presumably to establish whether they were likely to be an easy conquest or whether she'd get a boot for her trouble, and having decided, she would tailor her approach and either crawl forward on her belly or go sideways, very tentatively.

If they were encouraging and held out a hand or spoke to her, she'd get up, wag her tail and trot over, and then sit patiently waiting for her reward. She took everything that was offered, crusts of bread, bits of meat, chips, with or without tomato sauce, but I noticed that she didn't immediately gobble everything down.

She usually ate the meat straight away, but other things she would hold in her mouth. I saw one lady give her a burger bun, which she took with delicate precision. It was as if she didn't want to be rude and turn something down, but obviously burger buns weren't a hot favourite of hers, and she didn't immediately eat it.

Once the woman had turned away, she retreated to a safe distance and dropped it in the sand. She obviously wasn't starving then, I thought with a wry smile. She was almost certainly not in need of rescue, which was just as well!

Most of Sandra's family had come over for the wedding. The youngsters were staying in Rhodes old town within walking distance of the pubs and clubs. My husband Tony and I and his 14 year-old son Adam were staying in apartments close to the beach.

The day before our holiday ended, when I was stretched out on a sun lounger, catching up on my holiday reading, Sandra came running across.

'That stray dog's got puppies in a cave up in the rocks,' she said breathlessly.

'Has she?' I sat up, still not really wanting to get involved.

'Yes, and we need your help.' Sandra's voice grew more urgent. 'One of them has crawled away and it can't get back and the mother can't reach it.'

If it had crawled in one direction, I knew it could probably crawl back in the other, but nevertheless I sat up.

'Why do you need my help?'

'Because none of us can reach it either, but you've got long arms.'

Sandra waited expectantly. She knew she had me. Despite my best impressions of being aloof and heartless, she knew I wouldn't be able to ignore a puppy in distress. But, just in case, she added for good measure, 'The mother's crying and the pup's yipping. Come on, you're the only one who can help.'

I often think back to that moment and wonder if things would have been different if I'd been born with shorter arms. Sometimes life-changing events can be predetermined by the most incongruous of details!

The dog and her pups were in a hollowed-out kind of cave part way up the shallow sloping cliff. She had chosen a good place to have her litter, the floor was soft sand, and it was sheltered from the weather.

When we got there several other concerned holidaymakers had gathered, but like Sandra none of them could reach the pup. I peered into the darkened hollow and when my eyes had adjusted I could see it nosing blindly around. It was squeaking pitifully, but I couldn't reach it either – even with my long arms.

'We need something a bit longer,' I said. 'How about a child's plastic spade? I could probably reach the puppy with that.'

One was swiftly found and I discovered that if I

lay down on the rocks and leaned my arm as far into the hollow as it would go I could just touch the pup with the spade. Very gently, I scooped him back towards me. A few seconds later I was able to reunite him with his mother.

She gave him a good licking to welcome him back and thumped her tail on the sand. Not that she didn't have her work cut out already. I counted 13 puppies. Some were black, but most were brown like their mother.

The scattering of holidaymakers sighed with relief and went back to what they'd been doing. For a while I sat and watched the little canine family.

I was not going to get involved. I really was most definitely not going to get involved – but that night, Tony, Adam and I saved bits of meat from our dinner, and the following morning, armed with our serviette-wrapped packages, we were back on the beach.

We found ourselves at the back of a queue.

It turned out that several holidaymakers were concerned about the dog and her pups.

'They're ten days old,' a German lady told us. 'This is our second week; we were here when she had them.'

'We 'ave phone ze animal rescue,' proclaimed a Frenchman, throwing his hands in the air, palm up, 'but he do not come.'

'They look as though they're getting quite well fed,' remarked Tony. Adam and I nodded. The mother's breakfast so far consisted of tuna fish, carefully scraped from its can into a bowl, with a fillet steak topping. Suddenly our bits of left over meat seemed quite a mean offering.

'She is very well fed,' said the German lady, 'but that is now – next week the resort will close – it is end of the season. What will happen to her then? No one will be here to feed her.'

'Someone ought to do something,' chipped in a third holiday-maker. 'She will starve to death when the resort closes.'

I pictured the little brown dog trotting down to her breakfast bowl, day after day, and finding it empty. I pictured her waiting patiently for someone to come. I pictured the pups yipping for their mother, while she slowly grew weaker. (I'm a writer and sometimes I curse my overactive imagination). Even so, I couldn't see how the dog would survive without help. From that moment on I was involved.

CHAPTER TWO

The rescue

EARLIER IN THE WEEK we'd been shopping in Rhodes old town and we'd put money in a tin for an organisation called Rhodes Animal Welfare Society (RAWS) so I knew there was a rescue place on the island.

We tracked down their number and I phoned them. We'd been told it was run by an English lady, but I had to ring several times before I could get hold of her. I persevered and finally spoke with her the day before we were due to fly home.

'Yes, I know about these puppies. You are not the first person to call,' she said, 'And we are happy to come and get them in our van, but we cannot just go to an empty beach and hunt for them. We need someone to direct us.'

'When can you come?'

'Tomorrow afternoon is the first time the van will be available.'

My heart nose-dived. 'We're flying back tomorrow evening and we have to check in. Can't you come any earlier?'

'No, I'm afraid we won't have a van until tomorrow afternoon.'

'What if we bring them to you?' I said, thinking on my feet. 'Would you take them in – the mother and pups – if we bring them to the sanctuary?'

'Yes. We will, of course.'

'Can we bring them now?'

'No. I'm afraid we are just about to close.'

'Tomorrow morning then – we will bring them all to you then.'

'That is fine,' she agreed.

I put down the phone, feeling triumphant, and realised that Tony and Adam were both staring at me in amazement.

My long-suffering husband, who has been on the end of many of my dog rescue schemes, was shaking his head.

'How on earth are we going to do that?' he asked.

'We've got a hire car. We can find the place. We've got enough time before our flight.'

'We're supposed to be meeting everyone for a big family lunch tomorrow,' he pointed out reasonably.

'No one will mind. They all like dogs.' I was tempted to add that it was his family's fault I'd got involved in the first place, but I knew that wouldn't get me many brownie points.

'Besides,' he went on thoughtfully, 'you can't just pick them up and take them. The mother won't let you take her pups.'

'She might bite us,' Adam pointed out with irritating percipience. He was supposed to be on my side. 'She might be quite wild.'

I brushed their concerns aside. I might not have wanted to get involved, but now I was determined to see it through.

'We'll find a way of doing it. Sandra will help us. We'll need something to put the pups in so we can carry them.'

It was Adam who spotted the red plastic bread crate outside the shop next door to our apartment. 'Do you think we could use that?'

'Great idea.' I snatched it up. 'We'll put some newspaper and old towels in to make it more comfy.'

'When exactly are you planning this rescue expedition?' Tony's voice was disapproving.

'We'll go down to the beach first thing.' I beamed at him. 'It doesn't need to be too early. There isn't anyone at the sanctuary 'til ten.'

'We've got to get there though.' He looked at the address I'd written on a scrap of paper. 'This is across the other side of the island. Had you forgotten we're meeting everyone for lunch? And what about our plane?'

I might have known he'd be more interested in his stomach than he was in catching the plane. Tony's always been a foodie.

'It'll be fine.' I kissed him. He was still shaking his head, but I could see Adam was keen on the idea of a dog rescue. And I knew Tony would help us. He's as fond of dogs as I am.

My plan, such as it was, was haphazard. Adam was right, the mother dog might not be too keen to be enticed away from her pups, but she was always pretty hungry.

I would order a steak for dinner that night – that should be tempting enough to lure her away from her pups. She wasn't so shy that she wouldn't take food and I thought that we could probably park our hire car as close to the beach as we could and then tempt her to it by laying a trail of fillet steak pieces.

The following morning, armed with our bait and the bread crate, we set off on our mission. Tony was able to get pretty close with the car. I left the rear door open and then we went to find the mother dog and hoped she wouldn't already be too full of breakfast to be tempted away.

In fact, this plan very nearly worked. She came with me willingly enough, happily being rewarded for every 20 or so steps with a piece of steak, and we got within a few feet of the open rear door before she realised something was amiss.

I hoped that one last piece of steak placed in the foot well would persuade her to get in, which was, with hindsight, perhaps rather optimistic. She wanted that steak, but she was suspicious of the car. I wasn't surprised. She had probably never been in one before.

It would have been a simple enough task to just pick her up, she wasn't that big, maybe the size of a small Labrador, and she was desperately thin. But for her milk she'd have been skin and bone. But I was a little afraid she might bite me.

We reached a stalemate. Try as I might I couldn't get her to actually go in the car. 'Come on, sweetie,' I called. 'Just one more step.'

She sniffed the air hopefully. She craned her neck. She wrinkled her nose some more. She was very keen on that last piece of steak. I sneaked around behind her. Then just as she put a tentative paw onto the foot well I shoved her from behind and slammed the door.

She was in. I was sweating. It was very hot. No way could she stay in that car for long. I didn't dare open the windows more than a couple of inches in case she jumped out. In the end I persuaded Adam to sit with her, so we could leave the windows open – not that she seemed in a hurry to escape.

But we needed to get the pups pronto.

Actually, getting the pups was easy compared to getting Mum. By now a circle of holidaymakers had gathered. The German lady, the Frenchman, a couple of English holiday-makers and some Greeks. It was one of the Greeks who came over to ask what we were doing with the pups.

'You do good? Or you do bad?' he demanded.

Tony explained what we were doing and after that everyone was keen to help. Rather than climb across the rocks with the bread crate it was easier to pass the pups down. A chain of people spread out across the rocks – all different nationalities, we communicated in smiles and halting English beneath the burning sun.

The pups were passed with infinite care from hand to hand along the human chain to the foot of the cliffs. I swallowed an ache in my throat as I placed each one gently in the box.

You hear so much about people not caring. Yet there we were – an incongruous mix of strangers of all nationalities, bonded by one aim – to take this little family to safety.

When all 13 were in the box we got into the car. Tony and me in the front and Adam in the back with the pups and their mother. The rescue operation had taken nearly three-quarters of an hour and I wasn't too sure how long it would take us to find the sanctuary. The instructions had been vague.

We were about to drive away when the German lady ran across and banged on the window.

'Take this,' she shouted, as I wound it down a few inches. I realised she was shoving a handful of drachma through the gap. 'You give it to rescue place,' she shouted.

I nodded, too moved to speak.

The rescue centre turned out to be several miles along a dusty unmade road, with rocks littering the way and a scattering of stunted olive trees on either side. Once or twice I thought we'd have to turn back. We certainly couldn't be doing the hire car much good. It was in grave danger of being rattled and shaken to pieces. No doubt there was some clause in our hire contract about keeping it on proper roads. I dreaded to think what would happen if it conked out in the middle of nowhere.

'Are you sure this is the right way?' I asked Tony.

'Mmm,' he grunted, without looking at me.

In the back the little, brown dog dozed peacefully, as the scenery went by. I'd been worried she might try to escape or turn nasty, but she didn't seem very bothered by this strange turn of events. The pups were quiet too. They knew she was close by.

Finally, after almost an hour's drive, we drew up

outside a wire fence and the unmistakeable barking of a lot of dogs in close proximity. We had arrived but I must admit my first impressions of Rhodes Animal Welfare Society were not inspiring.

The high wire fence (which I later learned was to stop people breaking in and stealing dogs) made the place look more like a prison than a sanctuary.

Welfare did not seem a very apt description. I felt a shiver of trepidation.

Adam waited in the car with the dogs while Tony and I went into the tiny office. I was beginning to have the first thread of doubt. Had I acted maybe a tiny bit impulsively? I didn't know anything about this place. Maybe I should have left the dog and her pups where they were.

'Can I help you?' The woman behind the desk looked up impatiently.

I explained why we were there and her face broke into a smile.

'Yes, we have prepared a kennel for her. Do you think she'll come with you – or do we need a collar and leash?'

'I think she'll follow her pups, but maybe we should put a collar on her to be on the safe side?'

She fetched a collar, which had a bit of old rope attached and we went back to the car.

I put the collar on the dog, although there was no need, she followed me willingly enough. Adam and Tony carried the crate of puppies across the dirt floor to the waiting kennel, which was tiled and clean and already set up with a roomy basket, which made me feel better. Adam and Tony put the crate of pups on the floor just inside the mesh door.

There was a fresh bowl of water too, I saw with relief.

As we got to the kennel, the dog hesitated. It was as though she'd suddenly realised captivity was imminent. With a small whine she pulled back on the rope.

'Come on, girl.' The kennel maid took the rope and pulled her firmly into the kennel.

I took a step back as she clanged the gate behind me. I locked eyes with the dog and I saw her look of reproach.

I trusted you, and you've betrayed me. Her expression was clear.

It was crazy. I knew we were doing the best thing for her, but in that moment I felt like an utter Judas. My throat seized up and my eyes filled with tears. I wanted to run back into the kennel and gather her up in my arms and tell her it was going to be fine. Of course it was going to be fine.

But I didn't know that it was going to be fine.

'Do you think you'll be able to find homes for them?' Tony asked, as we handed over the drachma people had given us, along with a donation of our own.

Tony might have pretended he was indifferent,

but I knew he cared about the stray dog as much as I did.

'I hope we can find homes,' the kennel maid said. 'All I can tell you is that we will try our best.'

I nodded and thanked her, and then we had to go. There wasn't time to worry too much about the dog after that. We had to get a move on. We drove back towards civilisation – we'd missed our relaxed lunch with Sandra and Colin and the rest of Tony's family, but we could just about fit in a snack if we were quick before we needed to head for the airport.

We found a restaurant in Rhodes town and ordered pizzas, thinking that would be quicker. But it seemed the world and his wife had picked the same moment to have lunch. A harassed-looking waiter threaded his way through the packed tables, with plates held aloft, but our pizzas didn't materialise.

After about half an hour Tony said, 'We'll have to cancel our order if they don't come soon. We really should be getting going.'

I nodded, feeling guilty that what should have been a relaxed lunch with his family had turned into a stressed-out rush.

And then just as we were about to leave our pizzas arrived, or at least mine and Tony's did. Adam had to wait another five minutes for his. He had to wolf down the last of it while we paid the bill, and then we were on our way.

'Don't worry, we'll still be in plenty of time,' I said, as we drove up an oddly quiet road, which was signposted to the airport.

'Mmm.' Tony frowned. 'There's something wrong here.' He has an instinct for directions so I knew he was probably right. Although, exactly what was wrong didn't become apparent until we got to a *Road Closed* sign, beyond which stretched lines of bollards.

'Maybe we could ignore the sign,' I ventured. I've never been very conventional when it comes to rules.

'I don't think so.' Tony leapt out of the car, shielded his eyes from the sun and stared past the bollards into the distance. 'This is a new road. And by the look of it it's not finished yet.'

Back in the car he hunched over the map.

'Can't we just go back the way we came,' Adam asked.

'Not if we want to get to the airport on time. We'll have to take a detour.'

The next thing we knew he was heading down an unmade track, not dissimilar to the one that had led us to RAWS.

I knew better to ask him if he was sure this was the right way. Tony's sense of direction is legendary. And sure enough after an anxious 15 minutes we came out on to one of the main roads and picked up an airport sign. We were 10 kilometres away. Presuming there were no more hold ups we'd just about make it.

I think we all breathed a huge sigh of relief when we were finally on the plane home. As we soared away from the little island and through the eternally blue skies, my thoughts drifted back to our rescue mission.

Were the little brown dog and her pups really going to be OK? Had we freed them from the frying pan, only to throw them into the fire?

All I could do now was to keep my fingers crossed and pray.

CHAPTER THREE

Have I made things worse?

BACK HOME IN ENGLAND, I tried to put the little canine family out of my head. We had done the best we could for them. There was nothing more we could do. Absolutely nothing.

I kept telling myself this, but it made no difference. I was haunted by the look the mother had given me as the kennel door had clanged shut on her.

I trusted you. You betrayed me.

It was no good. However hard I tried I couldn't get her out of my head. A week went by and then a fortnight. I was still haunted by those eyes.

'I wonder how that dog and her pups are getting on,' I said to Tony. 'Do you think the sanctuary will be able to find them homes?'

'Yeah – course they will,' he murmured, looking

up from his paperwork, which he was doing at the lounge table, late one night. Tony and I were both self-employed, which tended to mean we worked long and unsociable hours. Fortunately, my job as a writer was home-based, which fitted in well with the dogs.

I looked at our dogs, all of whom were curled up on the settee, which meant there was no room for any people. At that time we had a white German Shepherd called Katie, a black collie cross called Jess, and a brown and white greyhound cross called Abel.

How sleek and well-fed they all looked, dozing amidst the cushions. My mind wandered back to the little brown dog in Rhodes. What a different life she'd had to my spoilt lot.

'I thought I might just email the sanctuary and ask how they're getting on,' I added.

Tony raised his eyebrows in affectionate exasperation. 'Good idea. It'll put your mind at rest.'

I sensed he was too immersed in his paperwork to be really listening and I decided there was no time like the present. I ran upstairs to the spare bedroom which I used as an office and emailed the sanctuary.

12 October, 2001
Dear RAWS,

We recently brought in a bitch with thirteen puppies that we found living wild in the rocks on Lindos Beach and I was wondering if you could tell me how they are getting on – and if there is any news on a home for them.

Many thanks

Very best wishes

Della Millward

The reply whizzed back sooner than I anticipated.

Tue 16 October, 2001

Dear Della Millward,

Rita in Denmark who keeps our website passed your message on to us here in Rhodes. The Lindos bitch is very well. I saw her today. She has a very sweet nature and gets on well with the other dogs at the kennels.

She is a wonderful mother and when she is free in the yard, she wants in to check her babies in the cage and then wants out again. She needs some time away from the babies although they are still not at the very demanding stage yet. She has actually taken on two pups from another bitch quite happily. The other bitch is very poorly with mastitis and an infection in her uterus.

Hopefully all the pups will be re-homed. The mother although she has a lovely nature will be difficult to re-home. We just have to wait and see

what happens.
Best Regards,
Maggie Avgerinou for RAWS

I kept reading that line, *the mother although she has a lovely nature will be difficult to re-home.* So what was going to happen to her then? Perhaps far from doing her a favour I had actually signed her death warrant. Did they mean they would have her put to sleep? The thought chilled me. But I was realistic enough to know that they might not have a choice.

All animal sanctuaries are run on tight budgets and only survive because of the dedication of animal lovers. I knew this because I helped out with fostering and dog walking for Dorset Animal Workers Group (DAWG), my local rescue centre. I also knew sanctuaries abroad have an even tougher time than the ones in the UK.

No sanctuary could afford to keep a dog indefinitely, which had no chance of being re-homed. I decided to talk to Tony about my worries that the dog wouldn't find a home.

'Maybe we could bring her back here,' I ventured.

He shook his head. 'Love, it will cost a fortune. We can't bring back a stray dog from Greece. We don't have that sort of money.'

'True,' I agreed.

Neither of us earned a massive amount and we had a big mortgage. I had a car that was on its last legs and had been saving up for ages to replace it. We definitely didn't have money to throw away on strays from Greece.

'Besides, we've already got three dogs,' Tony pointed out reasonably. 'Four would be too many.'

'Absolutely,' I agreed. So why did I find myself sitting down at my computer that night and typing another email to RAWS.

Tue October 16, 2001 9.10 pm
Dear Maggie,
Many thanks for your message. I'm pleased she is doing well and it's great that she has taken on two more pups. I would love to re-home the mother here in the UK.
I know this is difficult to arrange because of our quarantine regulations. I've been talking to a friend of mine, who deals with rescuing animals abroad, and she told me that also there is a shortage of MAFF vets in Greece, which makes it even harder. She thinks the easiest way to bring a dog back from Rhodes is to fly her to somewhere like Gibraltar, have her vaccinated and passported and then bring her back here, six months later.
Alternatively, she could be flown back and then put in quarantine here. I'm not sure which would be the most stressful for her.

I do realise that either of these options would be expensive, but that isn't a problem. If all this sounds too complicated to you, please say. In the meantime I will find out some more information about the practicalities.
Many thanks
Della Millward

I read the email back to myself and bit my lip when I got to the line about the expense not being a problem. Who was I trying to kid? Tony had already made it clear that we couldn't afford it. I *knew* we couldn't afford it. On the other hand I did have my car savings. Having a newer car surely wasn't as important as saving the life of a little Greek dog.

I convinced myself it wasn't, and, feeling only the merest flicker of guilt because I was going against Tony's wishes, I pressed SEND.

Maggie's reply came back before I had a chance to think through the implications of what I was doing.

Wed, October 17, 2001 16.44
Dear Della,
It is great to hear that you are considering taking Mummy dog back to UK. I didn't hold out much hope here of finding her a home, yet she has such a lovely character and such soft, sweet eyes.

We have sent 2 dogs and a cat this year to UK using the Pet Pilot scheme. Vaccinations, passport and micro chipping are all done by our local vet. Blood tests are done 30 days after the rabies vaccine, and that is a simple matter of sending the blood to Athens to be tested. Keeping the animals for seven months was a huge responsibility for us (dogs are stolen from the kennels, they can get into dog-fights, get sick, escape etc.)

The pet pilot scheme may be a bit cheaper. We have also sent a lot of animals straight into quarantine. That way at least the owner can visit the dog and it will be safer although it is more expensive. Also then, the animal can arrive into UK on any airline (scheduled)

You have to seriously consider your options, see what expenses it would involve. Let me know what you decide.

Best Wishes,

Maggie (Avgerinou)

I decided to have another chat with Tony. I knew he loved dogs as much as I did. I would appeal to his better nature and also I would reassure him that it wouldn't cost him a penny.

'About that Greek dog,' I began.

My timing was obviously not brilliant, because before I could get any further, he put his hands in the air, palms facing me and shook his head, 'I don't want to hear another word about that dog.'

'But I could afford to bring her back if I didn't buy a new car.'

'I'm not discussing it any more.' He walked away.

I sighed heavily. I knew he was right. It was a crazy idea.

I went upstairs and composed another email to Maggie.

Friday October 19, 2001
Dear Maggie,
I have decided that I will definitely go ahead and bring her back here to the UK. Give me a few days to look into things my end and I will be in touch again.
Many thanks for all your help with this
Very best wishes
Dellax

CHAPTER FOUR

Lindy comes to England

I DIDN'T DARE TELL Tony what I was up to. I wasn't in the habit of deceiving him, but I just couldn't live with the thought that I might have inadvertently made things worse for the little stray dog in Greece. I felt personally responsible for what happened to her.

For the next few days I corresponded with Maggie regularly. I decided to call the little dog, Lindy, after Lindos Beach where we'd found her. By coincidence Maggie decided to call her Lindy too – and in crossed emails we realised we had independently chosen the same name.

It seemed like a good omen! Although I think by then I'd have clung on to anything that indicated I may be making a good decision, rather than a very bad one!

Incidentally, we later discovered that we hadn't found her on Lindos Beach at all, but Pefkos Beach – I never have been good at geography – but by then it was too late to change her name!

Maggie said that while the sanctuary was quite happy to keep Lindy until she'd had her rabies vaccination and quarantine period and could come to the UK on a pet passport, they couldn't guarantee her safety. Dogs were sometimes stolen from the kennels, they had fights with other dogs, there were illnesses and sometimes dogs simply escaped and took their chances living wild. She thought it would be safer if I arranged quarantine for Lindy in the UK.

So I began to do some research. The kennels I found was near Salisbury, Wiltshire, which wasn't too far from where we lived. They said we could visit as often as we liked while Lindy was in quarantine, which was reassuring. They also said I could pay her bill monthly, which was a huge relief. I knew the quarantine cost would run into a couple of thousand pounds, possibly more, but at least I wouldn't have to pay it all at once.

Then I came up against a major stumbling block. Maggie had said that I needed to find an airline that would fly from Rhodes to Athens and then from Athens to Heathrow. It had to be an airline that would take dogs as cargo. It also needed to be the same airline so they could transfer Lindy from one plane to another. Maggie had mentioned I'd need a volunteer to go to Athens and make sure Lindy was transferred properly and not left sitting on the tarmac somewhere forgotten.

None of this was going to be easy. Then to make matters worse we discovered that no airline would take an unaccompanied dog between Rhodes and Athens. Someone would have to fly with Lindy for the first leg of the journey.

I panicked. For a couple of days I thought I might need to personally fly out to Rhodes and arrange to do this myself, which wasn't ideal because I didn't speak the language. And it would obviously also be quite a bit of extra expense.

And there was the small matter of what Tony would have to say about it. He'd already made it clear how he felt about the whole thing. The worry niggled away at me and I wondered, once more, if I should just give up this crazy idea of bringing Lindy back to England. Even though I knew I was already too involved.

Then to my very great relief Maggie offered to do it herself if I would pay for her flight, which of course went without saying. I could have hugged her. Once again it struck me that while there might be a lot of indifference to animals in the world, there are also some wonderful people around who will bend over backwards to help.

I hadn't even met Maggie, but she was willing to

go to extraordinary lengths for me and for Lindy. It still moves me to tears when I think about that.

As we made arrangements for the quarantine and the flight, Maggie kept me updated on Lindy's progress via email.

Tuesday October 23, 2001
Hi Della,
I saw Lindy on Tuesday. She came for a hug, big loving eyes but soooo thin. We are doing our best with vitamins extra food etc. but she obviously was undernourished before she was pregnant and it will take time to build her up again. A vet has looked at her and said she seems well but we don't want to neuter her yet, she is too run down, so maybe you can get that done in the UK.
She has an appointment with another vet to be micro chipped and given the rabies shot. I don't think this has to be done if she is going into quarantine, but it will cut down the time she has to be in quarantine as it counts exactly six months from the date of the rabies vaccine. He will give his opinion too as to her condition.
Can you confirm what she actually needs to get into the country, health wise, vaccine wise etc?
I am so relieved that this sweet dog is being given a chance in life. Thank you.
Best Wishes,
Maggie (Avgerinou)

I worried too about Lindy being run down and undernourished. I was responsible for moving her from that beach and for all that had happened to her since. But actually bringing her back to England was starting to feel like a reality.

Sunday November 4, 2001
Hi Maggie,
I sent the forms off to my kennels today, so hopefully you should hear from them within a week or so.
I took one of my dogs, Jess a collie cross, riding with me today. She had a great time running around in the forest and is now lying flat out by the fire. It's starting to get a bit cold here; frost on the ground, but Lindy's kennel is heated, so she'll be ok.
I've been trying not to look forward to seeing her in case things didn't work out, but am starting to hope now. This probably sounds mad, but she was so happy when I first saw her running along Lindos beach. I knew she couldn't survive there with all those pups, but I did feel a bit of a betrayer, taking her along to the kennels. I can't wait until she's here and through quarantine and I can let her run along an English beach. My three dogs love the beach.
Anyway, please let me know when you hear anything and what money you need me to send for

expenses etc
regards
Della

Monday November 5, 2001
Hi Della,
I don't think Lindy is too miserable up at the kennels. She is free in the yard every morning with the other dogs, whom she seems to get on with. She seems an easily satisfied dog, not a cowering one like a lot we get in, and very gentle and friendly. She will get to run on the beach again but this time with an owner who cares for her. She will be well fed and sleek-coated. That I would love to see, so a photo eventually would be much appreciated.
We separated her from the pups today, her milk has almost dried up and the pups are eating food now.
Let's see if she can get some weight on now.
So we wait for the papers to come!
Regards,
Maggie

There was a lot of official documentation to do for the flights and for the quarantine side of things, and there were obviously some translation problems between the UK and Greece. A few days later Maggie received the MAFF Boarding Document for Lindy. Under 'DESCRIPTION' someone had written:

Male, Lindy
16 years, brown.

We had in fact estimated Lindy to be between four and five years old, and she was patently not male! Her teats were still quite dangly and obvious! Maggie and I both laughed about this.

But finally, we got there. All the flights were arranged. The quarantine kennels were booked, the paperwork complete.

I had, by now, confessed all to Tony. Much to my relief he hadn't demanded an instant divorce. I knew he cared about dogs as much as I did – he just had a more sensible approach to the whole issue of animal rescue. Normal people put their spare change into animal-charity collecting boxes. Or if they were really passionate about a cause they did a sponsored walk. They didn't bring stray dogs back from Greek beaches.

I had never been particularly normal when it came to animals, but even I had to confess I'd followed my heart on this one and not my head. Still, it wasn't as if I'd planned it from the outset, was it!

Tony was also a little worried about how Lindy would get on with our other three dogs. I wasn't worried about this – I had a feeling that she would be fine. She'd seemed quite passive and laid back and Maggie had said she got on with the dogs at the kennels.

I promised Tony that if there was any trouble I would re-home Lindy when she got here – while keeping my fingers crossed that there wouldn't be. I also promised I'd cover all the expenses of bringing her back. Tony had no arguments left. In fact, as time went on the topic of Lindy often came up when we were talking to friends or at dinner parties, or just out with our dogs.

Tony would smile proudly and say, 'We brought this one back from Greece. She was living wild with her 13 pups on the beach.'

At first I used to correct him. '*Who* brought her back from Greece?' I'd ask him, and he'd just grin.

But I am getting ahead of myself.

Lindy finally flew back to England on a chilly grey day in November. The manager of the quarantine kennels phoned to let me know she'd arrived safely and that she was a bit cold so he would set up a special heat lamp in her kennels.

'You can come and visit her whenever you like,' he said with a smile in his voice. 'And I can also tell you her official release date is the 21st May.'

'That's amazing,' I told him, with a little shock of surprised pleasure. 'The 21st's my birthday.'

CHAPTER FIVE

Who's afraid of cows?

IT'S HARD TO SAY whether Lindy actually recognised us as being the 'betrayers who had lured her away from her beach' when we first visited her in quarantine. I suspect she didn't. And, actually, I didn't recognise her the first time I saw her either. Her ribs and backbone jutted through her dull brown coat. She looked woebegone and smaller than I remembered.

'I think they've sent us the wrong dog,' I said to Tony, as I fondled one long brown ear. 'This isn't her, is it?'

'I think it is her. I remember her having a torn ear.' Tony's always been more observant than me.

Her ear wasn't, in fact, torn, the edges were too neat – it looked more like her ear had been cut neatly with a knife – I'd heard that hunters often used knife marks to identify their dogs. I suspected that Lindy had once belonged to someone, who'd either abandoned her or perhaps just thrown her out to have her pups. I figured that if he'd wanted her he'd had every opportunity to collect her from the sanctuary and hadn't – so he obviously wasn't too bothered.

When we got back after that first visit to the quarantine kennels I checked the photos we'd taken of the dog on the beach. It was definitely Lindy – the same neat cut in the ear, and the same white spotty paws.

She'd been fat with milk when she'd been on that beach, but now her milk had gone I could see what poor condition she was in. The first thing we did was to arrange with the kennels for her to go on a special diet. They were as keen to build her up as we were.

'You won't recognise her by the time she's ready to leave,' they assured us, and they were right. Over the next six months Lindy filled out. Her coat became glossy, her eyes shiny. We went and visited her most Saturdays, we took treats and we stayed and played with her. When we left she didn't race around like the other dogs or bark, she sat proudly in her outdoor run with her chest sticking out, watching us go.

We hadn't seen Sandra and Colin since the wedding and we hadn't told them about bringing

Lindy back to England. Tony wanted to keep it a surprise and they lived in Nottingham so it wasn't difficult. But one day about three months after Lindy had gone into quarantine they came down to Dorset to stay with us for the weekend.

'Let's take them up to the kennels and surprise them,' Tony said. 'We can go to Salisbury shopping and you can pretend you have to nip into the kennels on some rescue mission.'

I regularly helped out dog charities so this wasn't too far fetched an idea.

Sandra and Colin suspected nothing. As far as they were concerned the dog on the beach in Rhodes was ancient history. Although they did know we'd taken the mother and her pups to the sanctuary.

We set off to Salisbury, having mentioned that I needed to drop off some dog food at a kennels en route. When we pulled into the car park, they pulled in alongside us.

Tony, Adam and I got out of the car, trying to hide our excitement. I couldn't wait to see Sandra's face when she realised what we'd done.

'Why don't you come in and have a look at the dogs,' Tony said casually.

Sandra didn't need any encouragement. A little troupe of us set off for Lindy's kennel. Sandra must have known something was going on when we went into the back entrance – the quarantine kennels had large runs on the front and you could walk through from the back. But she didn't actually realise what was happening until she saw Lindy.

'It's that dog,' she gasped. 'You've brought that blinking dog back from Rhodes.' And she promptly burst into tears.

Lindy must have wondered what on earth was going on, having two extra humans crying over her. It was a very emotional moment. Since that day in 2002 we've sprung several surprises on Sandra – but I don't think any of them have been quite as much fun as that one was!

The weeks went slowly by and then finally it was time for Lindy to come home, what a birthday present that was!

Tony, Adam and I went up to get her. She had already stolen our hearts by then. We were all a bit choked as we put on her new lead and led her out to the car for her first real taste of England. I wanted to take her to a beach. For the last few months I'd dreamed of seeing her run free on a beach in England. But in reality I knew it was best to let her settle down first. She needed to meet Katie, Abel and Jess and she needed to get her bearings.

Whichever way you looked at it her life was going to be very different from what it had been in Rhodes, or indeed from what it had been for the last six months.

She got on well with the other dogs straight away. Abel, our greyhound cross gave her a cursory sniff and then ignored her. Jess, our older collie cross did much the same, and Katie, our white German shepherd, wanted to play with her.

Lindy fitted in perfectly. On the surface she was submissive. She didn't encroach on the other dogs' territories at all, she didn't try and steal their food or take over their living areas, but I soon realised that she was extremely smart. She quickly worked out that the most comfortable place to sleep was the sofa and being on it as much as possible became her mission.

Abel and Jess had never been 'big' sofa dogs although Katie liked to sneak up there and as German shepherds take up quite a lot of room this didn't leave a lot of space for Lindy. However, she soon worked out a way to get Katie to move. She would stroll into the room, go into the middle of the floor or somewhere in clear sight of Katie and begin to paw at the carpet. Katie would jump off and go and see what was so interesting and Lindy would leap into the vacated spot.

After a while Katie worked out she was being conned and would refuse to move so Lindy devised several variations of her technique. Sometimes she would instigate play – Katie could rarely resist this. Sometimes she would lie on her back and wriggle madly from side to side like a little brown pig – we came to call this her wriggle-piggle manoeuvre – Katie could never resist this either. Or sometimes she would bark and race to the front door, whereupon Katie would follow her. By the time Katie discovered there was no one there it was too late, Lindy was already installed on the sofa.

And once she was in her spot she was impossible to move. If you tried to lift her off she would go 'floppy' suddenly becoming a dead weight in your arms. If you shouted at her she'd move but then she'd sit and stare accusingly at you from the carpet. When she figured that enough time had gone by she'd put up one front paw – if that went unnoticed she'd put up her second front paw – and if that went unnoticed she'd put up one hind paw until before you knew it she was back in situ.

It was easier to let her sleep up there. For a dog who'd lived wild on a beach she was surprisingly fond of her home comforts and she knew how to get what she wanted.

'I don't know why you're surprised,' Tony said, when I joked that Lindy knew exactly how to manipulate her canine companions. 'She manipulated you into bringing her back from Rhodes, didn't she? Getting a dog off the sofa must be child's play.'

For a while, we didn't let her off the lead when we took her for walks, I was scared she might run off and not know where she was, but I had to risk it sooner or later.

It was a Saturday morning in June and Adam and I and the three other dogs were out over the fields at Throop – we were near a river. It was very peaceful with just the lapping of water against the bank and the occasional squawk of a mallard for company. There was no one in sight as far as I could see, just a few cows a couple of fields along from us, but they were far enough away not to be a problem.

'She's so laid back I doubt she'll go far,' I said confidently as I bent to unclip her lead.

To my surprise and alarm the second she was free Lindy hurtled into the distance like a small brown cannonball. I had never seen her move so fast. At home she either slept or sauntered about, but now she was obviously on a mission.

Fear sent my heart into triple time. 'What if she never comes back?' I gasped to Adam. 'We might never see her again.'

He looked worried too. By now Lindy was a fast-moving dot in the distance. Abel had gone with her – that was something – at least I knew he'd come back when I called him – eventually!

It took me about three seconds to realise that the dogs were heading for the field of cows. Adam must have realised the same thing. We looked at each other in horror and we started to run at around the same moment that we heard a volley of frantic barking.

By the time we got to the field all we could see was a herd of stampeding cows. A black and white river of them poured across the grass – the thunder of cloven hooves was horrendous. I shielded my eyes against the June sun. About six feet in front of the herd – and travelling very fast – was a small brown speck of a dog.

It was Lindy – goodness knows where Abel had got to – but Lindy was in danger of being flattened by the stampede, which she had presumably instigated.

I yelled her name, but I doubt she heard. Adam and I clambered over the gate, but by now the cows were halfway across the next field. I prayed that they'd stop when they got to the barbed wire fence and not charge straight through it. I prayed that Lindy would escape unharmed. There was still no sign of Abel, and then I saw him trotting sheepishly back around the edge of the field, his pink tongue lolling and his long white legs spattered with mud – or possibly cow pats! He wagged his tail when he saw us. It was obvious he'd been having the time of his life.

I clipped on his lead and we went cautiously across the field, still calling Lindy's name.

'She's probably scared out of her wits,' Adam said. 'I bet she's never seen cows before.'

'She might not stop running and she won't know where she is.' My stomach crunched with worry. 'What if she gets on to a road? It's not like she'll have any road sense.' Although actually, with her background, she probably had more road sense than all our other dogs put together.

We reached the next stile and were mid-climb when I realised that Lindy was sitting waiting for us on the other side. With a cry of relief I called her name and she wagged her tail. She was hardly panting, which surprised me considering she'd been running for her life a few minutes earlier. But she obviously wasn't planning any further expeditions for the time being. She was quite happy to have her lead back on.

'What's all the fuss about?' her expression seemed to say: *I'm not scared of a few cows!*

Although I did notice that she gave cows a wide berth after that. Horses were fair game though. She'd bark at a horse if she saw one. I suspected that's what had happened with the cows. She'd also chase rabbits, squirrels and anything else that moved.

'Well, they said she was a hunting dog,' Tony murmured when he heard about her adventures. 'I guess she's just following her instincts.'

I took her to training classes after that. I'd taken all my dogs to the same classes – so it wasn't as though I didn't know how to train, but it was fun going to a weekly class. Lindy did exactly what I told her in the sessions. She loved getting treats, from her point of view I was her own personal doggie-treat vending machine. And it was simplicity itself to *sit, wait* and *lie down* on command.

Unfortunately, she wasn't as well behaved outside the class. She would come back when she was called – but only if there wasn't something more interesting going on. She had selective deafness. If she was chasing squirrels or rabbits or birds – she would ignore the recall command completely until she'd had enough.

Fortunately, for all her chasing tendencies she rarely caught anything. But I really shouldn't have been so surprised when she got into trouble with the mallards!

CHAPTER SIX

Of course she can swim – she's a dog!

WE WERE AT A different river, one that was quite close to our house when Lindy discovered ducks, and what fun it was to chase them. This time Katie was her partner in crime. Our other dogs knew perfectly well that ducks could fly and hence weren't worth chasing. But Katie was still young enough not to let this inconvenient fact bother her.

And so it seemed was Lindy. She'd actually once caught a pigeon when we were out walking. He'd been a little slow to take off and Lindy had sprung into the air and grabbed him in mid-flight. Fortunately, she hadn't hurt him, but it did make me realise what a good hunter she was.

I'd never had much to do with hunting dogs, but once when we were out for a pub lunch someone had come over to pet the dogs and had remarked that Lindy looked like a German shorthaired pointer. When I got home I looked up the breed on the internet and found he was right.

She had the same stocky build, the same chocolate-coloured coat and the same long floppy ears. No wonder the hunting instinct was in her blood. She'd probably also had to catch a good deal of her own food in Rhodes. Although holidaymakers had been feeding her on the beach she'd obviously had several litters of pups before we found her – and she'd managed to survive for the first five years of her life.

Anyway, on this particular morning Adam and I were out with the dogs. The river was quite low and there were a few mallards and moorhens about. While Abel pootled around on the bank, he didn't like getting his paws wet, Jess, Katie and Lindy went in for a drink.

And then Lindy saw the mallards. Instantly, she was after them, splashing through the shallow water and barking madly. Katie joined in and after a cursory, and ineffective, command to 'Pack That In', I left them to it. They couldn't actually catch any birds because the mallards were sensible enough to stay out of range. The water was shallow at this point in the river so there was no danger to the dogs. Katie got bored quite quickly, as I'd suspected she would, and was happy to come back to dry land.

Lindy, however, was a different matter. She was having a whale of a time. She charged up and down barking with excitement and completely deaf to my calls. The mallards seemed to be teasing her, taking off when she got close and landing a few feet ahead of her on the water, but still out of catching range.

This must have been frustrating. And then to my amazement, because Lindy had never been over-keen on water, she started to swim after one of them. She still had no hope of catching it, but now I was worried. The mallard with its blue and green head and yellow beak swam serenely along and Lindy's brown head bobbed determinedly after it.

She was out of her depth and although the river was shallow at this point it was much deeper a little further along.

I shouted at her to come back, but she was way too engrossed in the chase. Adam and I, complete with the rest of the dogs, ran along the river bank. As it bent round to the right we could see the current grew stronger.

'She'll be all right,' Adam said reassuringly. 'Dogs are good swimmers.' Which was just as well, because Lindy was now way out in the middle of the river, paddling after the mallard for all she was worth. I wasn't sure she'd be able to get back to the bank even if she wanted to, which she evidently didn't.

'I'll have to go after her,' I said to Adam, not

relishing the idea one bit. It probably wasn't deep enough to get out of my depth, but it was very cold, not to mention muddy and slippery. I'd had dealings with this river before. I'd once had to pull Katie out of it when she'd got stuck in some reeds, a bit further along.

'I don't suppose you fancy doing it?' I added hopefully.

'She's your dog.' Adam grinned at me. 'You're the one who brought her back from Greece.'

'I should have left her there,' I muttered as I stripped off my nice warm coat. I wanted something dry for later. I left Adam holding the dogs and ran a bit further along the river. Lindy was still happily swimming, although the mallard must have been nearly out of sight.

The river bent round to the right and I decided my best bet was to head her off downstream. With one last rueful look at my trainers, which would be ruined after this little expedition, I waded in. I hoped Lindy might abandon the chase and just come to me when she saw me in the water.

No such luck. She didn't even turn her head. The water was very cold. I felt its chill rising up around my knees and the bottom was a slippery gooey mass of mud. This was going to be such fun.

'Lindy,' I yelled again, aware of a couple of fishermen a few hundred yards upstream staring at me in amazement. 'Get back here, now!'

'It was possible to drown in a few feet of water,' I mused, as I slipped and slid after my errant hound, although it was highly unlikely.

'Lindy,' I shouted, the cold making my voice crosser than I'd intended – not that I wasn't cross, but I knew from experience that shrieking furiously at a dog does not entice it to come back to you.

I was in just over my knees before she turned towards me. I was too far away to see her expression, but I suspected she was probably surprised. Or perhaps she thought I'd come to help with the chase. Whatever she thought she'd evidently had enough of swimming – or the mallard had got too far out of sight and she'd lost interest – because she finally started to head in my direction.

'Good girl,' I called encouragingly. The current was strong. I could feel it pulling at my legs.

Although she was now heading for me she was getting swept away to the right, bit by bit. If I wasn't careful she would be swept right past me, and beyond the point where I was standing the river widened out and looked deep. I quickened my pace, almost fell over, and carried on shouting encouragement. Fortunately the lie of the land was on our side and although Lindy didn't make it to me she'd fetched up against a jutting-out bit of bank where an old tree overhung the water a couple of hundred feet on my right.

I splashed over to help her out. She was tired. It

was an effort to struggle up the slippery bank and she staggered a bit as she hit dry land and immediately started to shiver. She's never been over-struck on the cold.

'That serves you right,' I scolded, as she gave me a wistful little wag and shook a shower of river droplets from her coat. 'Repeat after me, Mallards can swim faster than dogs.'

She wagged her tail again and then threw up on the grass, mostly water that she'd swallowed in her haste.

Adam arrived with the other dogs. 'Is she OK? I bet it's freezing in there.' I could see he was having difficulty keeping a straight face as I squelched around on the grass. In the end he gave up and we both ended up laughing – me slightly hysterically.

'Dad is going to laugh his socks off when I tell him about this,' he added gleefully.

He was right. Later, in the comfort of our lounge, with Lindy curled up in her spot on the sofa, paws twitching as she dreamed – probably about mallards – we regaled Tony with the story of our river rescue.

He laughed uproariously, especially when we hammed it up and said that Lindy was close to drowning, and I was a superhero dog rescuer instead of a reluctant wader-in-up-to-her-knees.

'She hasn't told you the best bit yet, Dad,' Adam said, slanting a wicked glance in my direction. 'She wanted ME to go in and risk hypothermia, not to mention drowning, in order to rescue HER dog. How irresponsible is that?'

'They don't call us wicked stepmothers for nothing,' I said, throwing a cushion at him. 'Anyway it wasn't deep.'

'Cold though, I bet.' He threw the cushion back at me harder, and then doubled over with another fit of giggles.

'Seriously though,' I said. 'If she'd gone any further she might not have been so lucky. I wouldn't have fancied her chances if she'd got to the weir. I'll have to keep a closer eye on her.'

'You're going to need binoculars then,' Adam pointed out, which was true. Lindy wasn't the sort of dog that stayed close by on a walk.

Tony stroked her head thoughtfully. 'So you've used up another of your nine lives, have you, Lindy Lou. You want to be careful. It's only cats who have nine lives, you know!'

CHAPTER SEVEN

Another life gone

ONE OF THE THINGS I noticed about Lindy was that she learned from her experiences. She didn't stop chasing mallards, but she didn't attempt to swim after one again – much to my relief.

That didn't stop her hunting expeditions though. If there was anything to be found on a walk – no matter if it was dead or alive – she'd find it. Fortunately most of the things she brought back were dead. Or perhaps that should be unfortunately, as she wasn't at all choosey.

Once we caught her with a squirrel's tail. By the state of it the original owner had been dead for some time. In fact, he had probably been forest fodder weeks ago, but no self-respecting forest carnivore had bothered to eat his tail.

Lindy wasn't so picky. If it had once lived it

could be eaten, was her motto. She charged past me with part of the tail hanging out of her mouth.

I charged after her, as did Tony, Adam and Fran, a dog-walking friend, who was with us at the time.

None of us could catch her. Neither did our demands for her to 'drop it' get any reaction other than to encourage her to eat it faster. Bit by bit the whole manky, rotting squirrel's tail, fur and all, disappeared down her throat.

'I can't believe she ate that,' Fran remarked.

'It was rank,' Adam agreed. 'It must have been like eating a toilet brush.'

'She's going to be so ill,' Tony added.

She was not ill. She wasn't sick and there were no unpleasant after-effects over the next few days. I don't know how she did it. She must have had the digestive system of an ox.

On another memorable occasion we were out for a Sunday afternoon stroll with the dogs and were almost back at our car when we realised Lindy had disappeared.

'She must have found something,' Adam and I said in unison. That was usually why she disappeared.

We called her, we whistled, we waited. We were just about to retrace our steps when we saw her in the distance running along the path heading our way. Because it was Sunday afternoon there were lots of people around and several of them turned to look at Lindy as she trotted by. One or two pointed and then side-stepped away.

'She's got something in her mouth,' I observed, as she came into clearer viewing range. Not that I could see what she had, but it was the way she was running with her head held high to stop her precious cargo from dragging on the ground.

'Oh blimey,' Tony muttered, 'It looks big – is it a rabbit?'

A family with two children squealed in alarm as she trotted proudly past them. We waited in horrified fascination. But it wasn't until she was almost back with us that we could see what she'd got. She dropped it at our feet with a pleased wag, as if to say, *Check that out!*

It was a deer's head. She'd been carrying it by one ear and its swollen blue tongue lolled from the side of its mouth. It had obviously been shot by poachers – and the head removed from the body – and Lindy had just paraded it past a line of Sunday strollers. No wonder they'd been pointing!

We couldn't leave it lying in the car park – lots of families came over this bit of heath land. With a horrified grimace, Tony picked it up and tossed it over the fence into the deep thicket beyond. Lindy was not at all impressed when we then bundled her back into the car and made a swift exit.

It was a little while after the deer incident that I

noticed she had a lump on her hind leg. She'd had lumps and bumps before and the vet had always said they were fatty cysts so I wasn't unduly worried. But I took her along to the practice anyway to get it checked out.

'It's probably nothing to worry about,' our vet confirmed. 'But I think it's best if we remove it and send it off for analysis. Just to be on the safe side.'

She had the operation a week or so later. I went to pick her up and she wagged her tail and came groggily to meet us. She loved going to the vet's. She loved going anywhere there were people.

It seemed odd when you considered her background, but perhaps it wasn't so strange. She'd relied on people on the beach – and she'd obviously figured out that while there were some who couldn't be trusted, most of them were OK.

The lump had been sent off to be tested and a few days or so later the vet called us with the results.

'I'm afraid it was a malignant tumour, after all,' she said. 'The good news is that we got it all out and it's a slow-growing one. The bad news is that it might well pop up elsewhere on her body. So you are going to need to keep a close eye on her.'

It was a shock. We'd joked about Lindy having nine lives before, but I hadn't really thought about it that seriously. Because she was a cross breed which were usually quite healthy and because of her rough start on the beach I'd just assumed she'd be a tough little dog. I hadn't even got her insured. But suddenly it struck me how vulnerable she was.

For the next few months I panicked every time I felt anything on her body remotely resembling a lump and I was always rushing her to the vet. Much to my relief there was never anything wrong with her although going to the vet's so regularly did get quite expensive.

'We should probably get her insured,' Tony said. 'But I suppose they're going to exclude cancer anyway – as it's something she's had before.'

I agreed with him. 'Of course, she might get something else wrong with her,' I said, 'But it's unlikely isn't it? I think we'll risk it.'

That was a decision I would later come to regret.

CHAPTER EIGHT

Lost in the forest

IT SEEMED TO BE a time of trouble for our dogs. At the end of November 2004, Katie, who was ten, developed a condition called CDRM, which is a condition that German shepherds sometimes get. Although this is not a painful illness it's progressive and it slowly paralyses the dog's back legs. In Katie's case our vet thought there was something else wrong with her, as the illness progressed very rapidly. By December both her back legs were paralysed and she became very distressed and would cry every time she moved.

On Christmas Eve I made the very painful decision to have her put to sleep and I said goodbye to my beautiful Katie. She'd been a rescue dog, too, although she hadn't come from anywhere as exotic as Greece, she'd come from a place in Poole.

Lying on beach Rhodes, 2001

Lindy as we first saw her,
Rhodes, 2001

Lindy in Rhodes Animal Welfare
Sanctuary (RAWS), 2001

Lindy with her 13 puppies in RAWS

Della visits Lindy in quarantine in Salisbury, 2002

Lindy working on getting fatter, 2002

Lindy in quarantine, 2002

Home in Dorset, Lindy relaxes in the garden of her new home

Lindy and Della in garden, 2007

Lindy steals another dog's basket, 2004

Lindy and Della, 2007

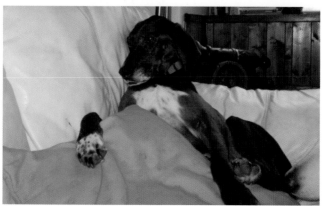
Lindy tired from steroids, 2007

Lindy in the garden, September 2007

Lindy in the garden, September 2007

Lindy and Della, 2007

Walkies! Maggie, Abel and Lindy, 2007

Della, Lindy and Maggie, Brecon Beacons, 2008

Lindy on holiday, Brecon Beacons, 2008

Della's husband Tony with Lindy

Lindy and Maggie,
November 2008

Cushion-shredding dog, 2009

Lindy plays with other dogs on
Chesil Beach, Dorset, 2009

Rosie, latest foster dog, 2009

How many dogs can you fit in your life?

Della with Tony's dog Seamus, 2010

Della with Seamus, Rosie, and Maggie, 2010

Life as a foster dog is tough, Rosie and Seamus, 2010

Although we still had Lindy, Jess and Abel, and although Tony and I had always joked that four dogs was one too many, Katie left a massive hole in my life. I was also painfully aware that all our dogs were getting elderly. Jess was 14, Abel, also a rescue, we thought was about 10, and Lindy was about 9. Not that she'd slowed down very much.

She still only had two speeds: flat out and stationary. And 18 months later when our next dog came along, Maggie, another white German shepherd, nothing much had changed.

Lindy taught Maggie everything she knew about chasing rabbits, which was quite a lot, and the two of them often hurtled off into the distance. Maggie wasn't as confident as Lindy and she usually came back pretty quickly but Lindy was very determined once she was on a scent and it wasn't unusual for her to disappear. However, I'd discovered that just because I couldn't see her, it didn't mean she couldn't see me. Most of the time she knew exactly where I was and she always caught up with me eventually. Consequently, I didn't worry too much when she ran off.

I knew she'd catch up in her own time. Once or twice when she'd misjudged where I was I'd found her waiting for me back at the car. The only time I really worried was when she and Maggie chased deer. Caught up in the thrill of the chase they would be oblivious to their surroundings and certainly deaf to my calls. Unfortunately, there were a lot of deer in Wareham forest and so it was an occupational hazard.

On one particular evening I'd been running with the dogs after work. Lindy liked running because we tended to go deeper into the forest, although I'd discovered that she wasn't keen on cycling because I'd be moving too fast and she couldn't calculate where I was going to be when she'd finished rooting about on her hunting expeditions.

She actually got so fed up of cycling that if she saw me put the bike in the car she'd run back in the house, as if to say, *No thanks. You can go by yourself.* And if I insisted on taking her she'd lie down on the path and refuse to move. I gave up taking her cycling in the end, although the other dogs loved it.

Anyway, on this particular evening we'd been running for about 15 minutes when Lindy and Maggie spotted three roe deer crossing the path ahead of us and shot off after them. Abel and Jess didn't bother to follow: Jess, because she was too old and Abel because he was too lazy.

I ran up to the point at which the dogs had left the path and whistled for them. We were a long way from the road so there wasn't much danger of them crossing it and risking injury and I knew the dogs had no chance of catching any deer so I wasn't too worried.

After about ten minutes Maggie came back, pink tongue lolling and her legs wobbly because she'd been charging around non-stop for too long. Maggie panicked if she couldn't find me – Lindy had no such qualms.

There was no sign of her and no sign of the deer. I did a circuit of the area, calling and whistling. After another 15 minutes I began to get a bit worried – Lindy would usually have come back by now, but there was still no sign of her.

It was summer and didn't get dark until nearly 9 p.m. so I still wasn't too worried, although I did phone Tony on my mobile and tell him what had happened.

'I'll drive up and help you look,' he offered. 'Whereabouts are you?'

I arranged to meet him in the car park and I headed back to the car in case Lindy had gone back there. But she hadn't.

A short while later Tony arrived and we searched for another hour keeping in touch on our mobiles. But Lindy had completely disappeared, swallowed up by the forest. To make matters worse the light was beginning to go.

I started to torment myself with visions of her lying hurt somewhere.

'What if she's got caught in a trap?'

'They don't have traps in Wareham forest,' Tony muttered.

'But something must have happened to her – or she'd have come back by now. I know she would.'

'Perhaps someone's found her and picked her up,' he said, which seemed the most rational explanation. Except that Lindy was wearing a collar and identity tag with my mobile phone number on.

'Wouldn't they have phoned me?'

'They might not have a phone with them.'

We carried on the search, but it was getting harder because we couldn't see anything. I didn't want to go home. I was still sure Lindy was out there somewhere and I felt that once we left the forest we'd be abandoning her. The thought of leaving her out there for the night was awful.

'We'll have to go home eventually,' Tony said, his eyes dark with concern. 'We can't stay here all night. And there's the faintest chance…' he hesitated.

'What?' I said.

'Well, there's the faintest chance she might have found her way home and be waiting for us.'

'But she'd have had to cross three main roads.'

'It's possible. You know what a little survivor she is.'

It was the possibility of this faint hope that persuaded me to give up the search – temporarily. We agreed that we'd be back first thing in the morning to continue it.

But Lindy was not waiting outside our house. I unlocked the front door and burst into tears. We might never see her again. The thought broke my heart.

She'd survived being abandoned on a beach, she'd survived a stampeding herd of cows, she'd narrowly escaped drowning and she'd fought off cancer. What if our beautiful feisty little dog had used up her stock of second chances? What if her lives had run out? What if we never saw her again?

Neither of us slept much that night. At first light we both stumbled out of bed and headed back to Wareham Forest to continue the search.

Maggie, Abel and Jess were delighted to be going out so early. In fact it was surprising how many people were out walking their dogs in the forest. But none of them had seen a little brown dog, with floppy ears and a pink collar.

While we searched I phoned up the police station to ask if any dogs had been picked up by the dog warden. I also phoned up our local radio station because I knew they had a lost pet slot.

Lindy couldn't just disappear into thin air. She had to be somewhere. I was just about to phone around my dog-loving friends to see if any of them were free to help with the search when my mobile rang.

'Yes,' I said breathlessly.

A man's voice said, 'Have you by any chance lost a little brown dog?'

'Yes. Is she OK? Where did you find her? Can I come and get her?' Suddenly aware that I wasn't giving him the chance to answer I paused.

'She's fine. We're in the Sherford Bridge car park. I'll wait here for you. I've got two Labradors.'

Tony and I ran all the way to the car park. When we got there we saw the man with two Labradors immediately, but there was no sign of Lindy.

'I'm sorry,' he said, wiping his face with a muddy hand. 'I was holding her by the collar but she was really anxious to get away and I lost my grip. She ran back up into the forest.'

By now I was crying, half with frustration and half with relief.

'At least she's OK,' Tony reassured.

In my pocket my mobile trilled again.

'I've found a dog.' This time it was a woman's voice. 'She's quite tired; I think she's been running a lot.'

'Where are you?' I gasped.

'Lawson's Clump car park.' Lawson's Clump was the next car park along the road from this one, about half a mile away, and was in fact where we'd come from. So she'd run all the way back there in the time we'd taken getting here – I was surprised we hadn't passed each other on the way.

'Please can you hold on to her? Please don't let her go,' I begged the woman. 'She's been out all night.'

'No worries,' she said cheerfully. 'I'll shut her in my car. It's a yellow Escort.'

Ten minutes later we were reunited with our little lost dog. She was extremely pleased to see us. She was also covered in mud and had a cut on her paw – so it had been very good of her latest rescuer to shut her in her car.

'I'm sorry; I hope she hasn't made too much mess.'

'Don't worry. I've got my own.' She indicated an elderly Westie curled up on a blanket on the back seat. 'I'm happy to help.'

Once again it struck me how nice people were.

With our doggie family complete once more, Tony and I headed for home. After breakfast and a shower he went off to work and I took Lindy to the vet's yet again to get her checked over.

She was none the worse for her night in the forest. Although she did sleep a lot that day. And it didn't stop her chasing deer either, but perhaps it made her more careful because to my very great relief I never lost her again.

CHAPTER NINE

Another battle!

IN MAY, 2007, SANDRA and Colin came to stay with us for the weekend. They'd lost their old black Labrador, Jet, the year before and they'd just got a new puppy. She was a boxer called Indy and they brought her down to show us.

Indy got on well with all our dogs and we spent the weekend going for long walks in the forest and eating out at pubs that let dogs in. Every time we called Indy, Lindy came and vice versa!

On the Saturday night I noticed that Lindy didn't eat very much of her dinner. She'd seemed a bit quiet all day, but I wasn't unduly worried. She didn't have a big appetite at the best of times and I suspected that her nose had been put out of joint by the puppy. I should have known better. Lindy got on really well with everyone, whether they were canine or human.

We headed off for a walk on Sunday morning and Lindy wasn't all that keen to come with us. Alarm bells had started to ring, but I still thought that the problem was the new puppy.

'You don't think she's ill, do you?' Sandra asked as we walked along the shady forest paths with Lindy idling along behind us.

I shook my head. 'Maybe – but I don't think so. If she's still off her food tomorrow I'll take her to the vet's.'

Later that afternoon, Sandra and Colin said their goodbyes and set off for home and I gave Lindy her dinner. Again she picked at it and I decided to take her to the vets the following morning.

But on Monday when I came downstairs Lindy got out of her basket and then collapsed at my feet. Horrified, I shouted for Tony and phoned the vet.

'We can see her at 10.15 a.m.' the receptionist said.

'I need to bring her now,' I gasped. 'I think she's dying.' I could hardly say the words. I felt terrible. Why on earth hadn't I realised she was ill? Why had I made stupid assumptions about her being jealous? The guilt bit deep.

Lindy couldn't walk. She couldn't even stand up. Tony carried her out to the car and we raced down to the vet's.

My little dog still managed a wag as we lifted her

onto the table for Kate, our vet, who is one of the nicest people I know.

'I'm afraid this looks serious,' Kate told us, having examined Lindy carefully. 'I need to wait for the blood test results to be sure, but I suspect she has something called haemolytic anaemia.'

Tony and I looked at her blankly.

'It is an auto-immune condition,' she explained. 'The white blood cells attack the red blood cells resulting in severe anaemia.' Kate lifted up Lindy's lip and showed us her gums.

'Look how pale she is. Her gums should be a healthy pink.'

I nodded. I'd thought I'd known a lot about dogs but I hadn't known this simple check.

'There are a number of causes,' Kate went on. 'Sometimes it's sparked by an inoculation, but often we never find out why it's happened.'

'Will she be OK?' There was a huge ache in my throat and I was trying not to cry. I had a feeling I already knew the answer.

'I have to tell you that the prognosis is poor,' she said, her eyes compassionate. 'We will start treating her straight away. I won't wait for the blood tests. I'm pretty sure she has this disease. I have actually seen four dogs with it recently.'

'What happened to the other dogs?' Tony asked.

'I'm afraid they all died. But that doesn't mean Lindy will die.' She stroked our dog's head and she got another sad little wag in response. 'She is a little fighter, aren't you, my love.'

For the next few days Lindy's life hung in the balance. She was on a drip, being given steroids and fluids intravenously, but she wouldn't eat anything. It was as though she was fading before our eyes.

The animal hospital was a room lined with sturdy metal kennels, each with its own bedding and bowl of water. It was where animals recuperated after operations and where the very ill ones were kept under close observation. Lindy was the only occupant at that time, although she had plenty of company. The vet nurses knew her well and loved her, and either Tony or I went in to see her daily. We took her in treats to tempt her: fresh-cooked chicken and bits of beef or steak. I hand fed her like I'd done on the beach six years earlier. She ate very little – she wasn't touching the food the vet nurses gave her either. Although she still managed to wag her tail.

On the Friday evening Kate called me on the phone. 'I think you should come in and see Lindy.' Her voice was grave. 'She is quite weak and she is not responding to treatment.'

Although she didn't say it I knew what she was telling me. My beautiful little dog had all but given up the battle. I would be going in to say my goodbyes.

I took chicken as I always did, but this time Lindy didn't even raise her head to sniff it. She just lay on her side although she had managed a weak little wag when she saw me. I couldn't help myself. I kneeled in her kennel and I cried my heart out, my tears falling onto her soft coat.

I thought of her as I'd first seen her, running on the beach, I thought of all the things she'd survived in her life: fending for herself and her pups on the beach; the stampeding cows; the river; the cancer; the night in the forest.

Was this it? Had she had her last life? Was it all to end here in this sterile little kennel? I didn't want to cry. I knew she would know I was upset but I couldn't' seem to stop. For a long while I sat and stroked her, still on my knees, her head in my lap, remembering.

But I couldn't stay there for ever. Eventually I laid Lindy's head back gently on the blanket and I got stiffly to my feet. I still had the roast chicken in my hand too. Lindy had refused it.

And then, just as I got up Lindy lifted her head and sniffed the air. I hesitated. It was as if she was saying, *Hang on a sec – maybe I could just manage a piece of chicken, after all.*

I went back to her side and held a piece out and she ate it. She didn't eat much, but it was a start. Suddenly I knew she had turned a corner. She had been very close to death, but she was still fighting. My little dog hadn't quite used up her stock of nine lives.

I was right. From that day on, Lindy began to improve. She started to eat again and she grew stronger. Bit by bit she fought her way back to health. A week later we took her home. She was on steroids for months and months. It was not an easy battle. The steroids made her thirsty and hungry and she put on masses of weight. We weaned her off the steroids very slowly, but every time we stopped them completely she started to go downhill again.

Slowly, slowly she recovered, and eventually she was free of steroids. She had beaten haemolytic anaemia, at least for now. Kate told us it could recur any time. She showed me how to check Lindy's gums to make sure they were the right colour; a healthy pink. She also told us that since Lindy had recovered, she had diagnosed another two dogs with the same disease.

'Were they OK?' I asked, even though, once again, I had a feeling I already knew the answer.

'No, they were not. Both of them subsequently died.'

I knew we were incredibly lucky that Lindy had survived. She also seemed none the worse for the experience. She still loved her walks. She still loved to chase things, although she was calming down a little bit as she grew older and she tended to spend more of her time finding dead things and eating them if she could get away with it. She frequently found bones when we were out. If ever she didn't come back when we called it was usually because she'd made some exciting new discovery.

We estimated that she must be about ten or eleven. Her muzzle was now quite grey – but life was good again.

Even though occasionally I realised she was living on borrowed time, I tried not to let it interfere with our enjoyment of now. When I'd first made the decision to bring Lindy back from Rhodes to live with us in England I'd predicted that she would bring a great deal of joy into our lives. And she had. I hoped we would have her for a few years longer.

CHAPTER TEN

I'm sure I shut the door

ALTHOUGH WE'D NOW MOVED to a village and there were lots of footpaths around us, it wasn't the best place to walk dogs because most of the footpaths ran across fields containing livestock.

Knowing Lindy's penchant for chasing things it was simpler to walk her elsewhere. So I tended to put all the dogs in the car and drive them out to Wareham Forest which wasn't too far from us.

Lindy now seemed to be fully recovered from the haemolytic anaemia. She was finally off steroids, she'd lost her excess weight and was enjoying her walks again. Even so, I was forever checking her gums. If she seemed quiet or if she lost her appetite I would worry.

If she got the slightest lump or bump I would worry too and would race her down the vets to get her checked out. Surprisingly she loved going to the vet's and they loved her.

After the haemolytic anaemia I'd had to take her for endless check-ups, most of which involved a blood test. By rights she should have hated going to the vet's and having needles stuck in her, but she didn't. When we sat in the waiting room the silence would be punctuated by the thump thump, thump of her tail against the tiled floor.

But all seemed well. I began to hope again. We were going to have her for a while longer.

One morning when I was driving back from Wareham Forest, having just been out for my walk with the dogs and no doubt dreaming of something else, I glanced in my rear view mirror and saw a dog standing in the road. I was on the A31, which is notoriously busy.

In the next heartbeat I realised that it wasn't just any dog. It was Lindy. And then I realised that my hatchback had flown open. The other dogs were still in the car – they obviously hadn't been sitting too close to the door, but Lindy had a habit of leaning against it.

Horrified, I pulled over to the side of the road and ran round to the back of the car. I was anxious to get Lindy out of the road, but I had to close the hatchback pronto, or I'd have had more dogs roaming around the busy road.

Fortunately the car behind me had also stopped

and there wasn't a huge amount of traffic around at that time in the morning. The driver, a man, was heading towards Lindy, who just stood there quite patiently, albeit a bit bemused, as though she knew someone would soon be along to rescue her.

The man grabbed hold of Lindy's collar and led her to the side of the road where I gratefully checked her over. She was fine – none the worse for her experience. Luckily I hadn't been driving too fast, but it could have been a very different story.

I was shaking a little from shock and the man was not impressed at all. It must have been a shock for him too seeing a dog fly out of the car in front of him. He obviously thought I hadn't shut the door properly. And I thought that too until later when I got home and Tony checked the catch.

'It's broken,' he said. 'It wasn't your fault, love; don't beat yourself up about it.' Tony is the kind of person who'd have said that even if it wasn't true just to make me feel better.

But as it happened he was right. My faithful old Toyota had done over a hundred thousand miles. Its bodywork was pretty battle-scarred and its front passenger seat had all but disintegrated.

That had been Lindy's work too, as it happened. She liked her home comforts and she also liked to make a dip in things if she was lying on them. To this end she had chewed a hole in the passenger seat, pulled out most of the stuffing and made herself a nice comfy dip in the middle of the seat.

I didn't bother to get the lock repaired. Six years after I had first planned to change my car, I took the Toyota off to the great scrap yard in the sky. I was quite sad to see it go, but we replaced it with a newer estate car – one of the first things I did was to have a dog guard fitted so that Lindy wouldn't be able to wreck the seats. She was most disappointed.

It was also the kind of car which had a light come up on the dashboard to alert you if a door wasn't properly closed. That was a big comfort to me. Never again would I be able to drive off with a door still open.

In 2007 Tony and I finally decided it was time to let Jess, our collie cross go. She was 16 years old, not a bad age for a dog, and for the last year or so of her life, she had been incontinent. We had tried numerous remedies from the vet's but I don't think it was a physical problem.

I think she had lost the plot. Jess had always been a very clean dog, she wouldn't dream of wetting in the house unless she was desperate, but now quite often she would wee on the kitchen floor – even if the back door was open and she could easily have strolled another couple of feet.

She would look at me quite happily as she squatted, as though she thought it was perfectly acceptable and I realised that she didn't know where she was. Because of this, and because I knew she wasn't mortified about her inappropriate wetting – on the contrary, she didn't know she was doing it – I saw no reason to have her put to sleep.

She still had a good quality of life. She still enjoyed her food and her walks. I invested in an indoor kennel which had a plastic base, and which was where she slept at night. Every night she wet her bed and every morning I washed her bedding and dried it ready for the following night.

This was time-consuming, but it was not a big chore, I decided, for a dog who had been a loyal and faithful companion for nearly half my life. The downside, of course, was that I knew Jess wasn't going to get better. Slowly, slowly, she started to get wobbly on her legs and slowly, slowly her life began to close in.

In my heart I wished often that I would come down one morning and find that she'd died in her sleep. I knew it was cowardice because I didn't want to make the final decision. It had broken my heart having Katie put to sleep, even though she'd been terribly distressed, and suffering an incurable disease and it had been the only kind way.

But of course I knew we couldn't let Jess linger on once her quality of life had gone. We discussed it with Kate each time we took her in for a check-up. It's always hard to judge when the right time is.

But one morning Tony and I decided it was time. Jess no longer enjoyed her walks. She was too wobbly on her feet and once or twice lately I'd had to help her get up. I knew I couldn't wait any longer.

Tony and I took her for her last walk. It was a beautiful sunny day and we picked a little-used forest walk. Tony lifted her out of the car and set her down on the path. She didn't go very far, just sniffed around a bit where she could smell other dogs had been. I was doing my best not to cry – I didn't want Jess to pick up on my sadness – but it was difficult. My throat was raw with the effort of swallowing tears.

And then we drove to the vets. I waited outside in the car with Jess while Tony went in and told them I'd stay there until they were ready. I couldn't have sat in the waiting room, listening to the chatter of the other owners who would no doubt be bringing along puppies for their vaccinations and cats to have their teeth cleaned and chatting happily about their animals in the way people do in vet's waiting rooms.

Once again, Kate was wonderful. She let us spend a long time in her consulting room. We talked about Jess and how she had been and what a wonderful life she had had – she'd been a rescue dog too from a tiny little animal sanctuary in Dorset. I'd had her since she was seven months old.

And then finally Kate administered the anaesthetic and Jess slipped away from us as we held her. I knew it was the right thing to do but another little piece of my heart broke.

I once read somewhere that the difference between a person you love and a dog you love is that a person has the capacity to break your heart many times, but a dog will only ever do it once.

How true that saying is.

CHAPTER ELEVEN

Rat poison and blackbirds

SO NOW WE WERE back to having three dogs again. Maggie was the only young one, but they all got on well. The one thing they all had in common was their love of food, although Lindy was the only one who'd actively seek it out. She was forever scavenging about to see what she could find. The deader the better, although things didn't have to be dead for her to take an interest. She just wasn't as quick on her feet as she'd once been.

One evening recently I'd been putting on my make-up in the bathroom – as well as being a writer I teach creative writing and I had a class that night – when I heard a kerfuffle downstairs.

I'd only just put the dogs outside to eat their dinner, and I'd shut the back door, but Maggie, who's rather good at doors, had obviously opened it again and let them all in.

The thunder of paws on the stairs alerted me to the fact that Lindy was en route to my office. She had a basket under the fan heater, which was on the wall, and would happily curl up in it while I was working.

With mascara brush in hand I ran along the landing to shoo her out again, I wanted the dogs to go out in the garden because I was leaving them alone for a couple of hours and I wasn't sure what time Tony would be back in to let them out again. Lindy was sitting in her basket. She wagged her tail and looked guilty, which wasn't surprising, as she had a young blackbird in her mouth. She was holding it by the tip of one wing and the rest of it was dangling down from her mouth.

She must have read my body language and known I wasn't happy because she shot out of her basket, and still carrying the poor blackbird, ran back down the stairs again. I was in hot pursuit. When I got to the dining room I saw that she'd dropped the blackbird on the floor.

It was younger than I'd thought, scarcely more than a baby and couldn't have had its feathers that long. The poor thing was obviously shocked but it looked up at me and opened its beak, as if expecting to be fed.

I locked the dogs in another room and carefully checked the bird. Amazingly it seemed undamaged, although I knew they could die of shock. I wondered where it had come from – I guessed it had only recently left the nest, and was perhaps having its first flying lessons, and its parents might very well still be around.

Making sure the dogs were locked in the house, I carefully picked up the blackbird, carried it out to the back garden and set it down carefully in the middle of the lawn. I was a bit worried. If it stayed there long it would be extremely vulnerable to cats or any passing foxes, but I wasn't sure what else to do.

Back in the house, I watched from an upstairs window. To my great delight another blackbird flew down and landed on the fence a few feet away from the young one. This was soon joined by a second bird. After making sure there was no apparent danger they flew down to the baby on the grass.

For a little while they fluttered around it, as if encouraging it to fly. Up and down they flew. I watched them for several minutes. I was going to be late for work but I wanted to make sure there was a happy ending. And finally there was. The young bird seemed to get the message and he took off with the parents and away they all flew.

I went off to my evening class feeling content with the world. It wasn't until I got home that Tony asked me what had been going on outside in our back yard.

'What do you mean?' I asked puzzled, as I hadn't yet told him about the incident.

'Well, I found the remains of something out there. Some innards and a bird's claw and some black feathers. It looked like one of the dogs had eaten a bird.'

'Oh,' I said, suddenly deflated, and then I told him what had happened earlier. 'The one I found definitely wasn't missing a claw,' I said.

'I guess there must have been two of them then,' Tony replied. We looked at each other. It was hard to believe that Lindy had eaten a live blackbird, but there didn't seem to be any other explanation.

Maybe the other dogs had helped her. It also seemed odd that two young birds had both fallen into our back yard at the same time. A gate separated the yard from the back garden, but that had been closed.

The mystery did in fact get solved a few weeks later. Tony had propped up last year's Christmas tree by the fence at the side of the house. And we found a nest about halfway up the five foot tree. Inadvertently, the parent birds had picked the most unsafe place in the world to raise their family.

I'm amazed that neither we nor the dogs had noticed the nest and its family before. That young blackbird had been even luckier than I'd first thought. The whole family had evidently abandoned the nest after the incident and had found a safer place to live. And Tony took the old tree down to the council tip to make sure it couldn't happen again.

I knew we would be less lax about getting rid of our old Christmas trees in future, but I am still amazed by that incident, both at the blackbird's fatal decision to build a nest in a Christmas tree and at Lindy's ability to eat almost anything.

A few months later, her penchant for eating rubbish was very nearly her downfall. We have an old lean-to-cum-wood-store next door to our kitchen. It's where we keep our freezer and our bikes and the car boot sale stuff I sell to raise money for DAWG.

The previous year we'd had a bit of a problem with rats. They got into the rafters of our old house and sometimes I had heard them skittering about in the joists. Also, once, I'd gone out to the wood-store and come face to face with one sitting on the logs.

I don't mind rats, but I was not at all keen on sharing my house with them, so we'd put out some rat poison in little trays high up on the upright freezer and out of reach of the dogs.

One evening, I was just out there getting something out of the freezer for dinner when I heard the phone ring in the house. I raced in to answer it, leaving the door to the wood-store open.

When I got back downstairs I saw that the dogs had taken advantage of the situation to have a root around in the wood-store. This wouldn't usually be a problem, but then I saw that Lindy had something in her mouth. When I asked her to give it to me she obliged with a wag of her tail and I saw to my horror that it was one of the plastic trays that we'd used to put rat poison in.

It must have been knocked off the freezer – presumably by a rat – but the burning question in my mind, was had it still contained poison? And if it had, had the dogs eaten any? All of them were milling about out there.

None of the blue pellets lay on the ground. I knew it was pretty unlikely that there had been any poison left in the tray, but I couldn't take the risk. I phoned the vets.

'Bring them down,' Kate said. 'We'd better err on the side of caution.'

So off we all went to the vets where Lindy, Maggie and Abel were given emetics to make them sick.

'I think she has just used up another of her nine lives,' I joked to one of the receptionists who knew Lindy well.

'I think you're right,' she said, stroking Lindy's soft brown ears. 'How many is it now?'

I didn't answer her, but later that night, I ticked them off on my fingers: number one was the beach rescue; number two was probably the rescue mission that had brought her back to England; three was the herd of cows; four was the river; five was the cancer; six was the forest; seven was the haemolytic anaemia; eight the dodgy catch on the Toyota; nine the rat poison. She'd had nine lives already. I looked at her curled up on the settee, with not a care in the world. I decided to stop torturing myself.

CHAPTER TWELVE

So this is goodbye

TOWARDS THE END OF 2008 we'd lost Abel. The end had come quickly for him. He'd been perfectly fine, eating and drinking as normal, and then he'd had a seizure one Friday evening. Luckily Tony and I were both home so we were able to comfort him and be there for him, and the on-call vet thought that he might well recover, but sadly it wasn't to be. We said goodbye to one of the sweetest-natured dogs we had ever had the pleasure to live with.

It felt very strange only having two dogs in the house. It was oddly quiet and very tidy. Once the novelty of not having to clean and vacuum so much wore off, I realised that I didn't like only having two dogs around. I wasn't sure we were ready for another dog of our own – we had to heal first – but

I thought I would quite like to foster a dog again.

We had fostered in the past for DAWG and so I phoned Helen, who runs it, and asked her to keep us in mind next time she was in need of a foster carer.

A few weeks later, Helen contacted me and asked me if I'd look after Max, a young collie she'd just picked up from a sanctuary in Ireland. She had several people interested in him, which meant it would probably only be a very short term fostering.

And so Max came to stay. To say he was scared would be an understatement. He'd never lived in a house before – he'd come from a farm in Ireland, where apparently he'd spent most of his short life tied to a gate. On his first day he wouldn't come inside. He sat at the back door gazing in at us, but he wouldn't step over the threshold.

When I wanted to get him in I'd have to go outside and kind of herd him in. After a few days he began to trust me a little more, but he still wouldn't come into the house unless I was standing well clear of the doorway. Then he'd shoot in at top speed and sit on my foot.

'It's so you can't kick him,' Tony said. He was only half joking. Poor Max had come from a background where he'd swiftly learned that human feet were to be avoided.

In fact, his previous owners had phoned up the

sanctuary in Ireland and said, 'If you don't take this dog, we're chucking it over a cliff.'

Nice people!

But actually they probably weren't too bad as ex-owners go. At least they phoned up the sanctuary and didn't carry out their threat. I was so glad they had. Max was the most adorable dog. I fell in love with him almost immediately and so did Tony.

Lindy took him under her wing too. She was a great dog to have around with foster dogs. She was maternal and calm and infinitely gentle with them. She showed them what was what, she demonstrated that our laps were a good place to be, as was the sofa, and that it wasn't necessary to bolt your food – or indeed to steal hers – because there was plenty to go around. And little by little they got used to the routines of the house and they learned to trust.

It has always amazed me how forgiving dogs are. No matter what they have gone through in the past they are always ready to believe that things can get better. I have learned an awful lot from dogs.

Anyway, as Helen had said, lots of people were interested in re homing Max. The perfect home came along very quickly. A couple called Andrew and Dominique who had lost their collie the previous year were looking for another one. They had been looking for a while – they didn't want a replacement but they wanted a dog who really needed love. They had no children, Andrew worked from home, they went walking in their spare time, and they were obviously avid dog lovers.

If they hadn't been absolutely the perfect home for Max I wouldn't have let him go – I'd have kept him myself. Tony and I were both besotted with him. But, as Helen so wisely pointed out, I could help a lot more dogs if I let Max go. I cried quite a bit when he went, but actually we do still see him and occasionally he comes to stay with us for his holidays – so we had the best of both worlds.

One sunny afternoon a couple of weeks later Helen phoned me again. 'I'd like you to foster Rosie for a while. She's another difficult one. She came from a horrendous background – it's probably best if I don't tell you what the owners used to do to her – suffice to say she's a terrified little dog and needs a quiet home to recuperate.'

Rosie turned out to be a rather beautiful brindle-coloured Staffie mix. She probably had some greyhound in her too – she had long legs and a slender body but her head was unmistakeably Staffie.

Helen was right. Rosie was even more terrified than Max had been. For her first few days she cowered in the indoor dog kennel and wouldn't come out. I left her to it, although of course she had to come out to do her business. Being near a human was obviously very traumatic for her, but fortunately she took to Lindy instantly and very soon the two of them were inseparable.

Lindy showed Rosie the ropes of the house, just as she'd done with Max. She showed her where the sofa was and how to curl up so tightly no one would notice you were on it. And also, as Rosie grew more confident, how to make yourself floppy and heavy so no one could throw you off.

Lindy taught Rosie that my office at the top of the house was a great place to be during the day – Lindy had her day basket under the fan heater on the wall. Rosie began to curl up with Lindy so I took another basket upstairs, but generally Rosie preferred to snuggle up close to Lindy so in the end I just got them a bigger basket.

Lindy also taught Rosie to follow me around, and so I had two shadows instead of one. I'm not sure if she also taught her how to empty the bin while I was out of the room or whether Rosie worked that one out for herself, but I would often find the pair of them sitting amidst shredded chocolate wrappers, which had hitherto been in the bin, when I got back to my desk with a cup of coffee.

Not that I sit in my office and eat chocolate all day, you understand!

Rosie was similar to Lindy in lots of ways. Both of them liked to hunt rabbits, although Lindy wasn't up to chasing them very far these days. Both of them had selective hearing when they were doing something 'very interesting' both of them liked to be a field or so away from me on walks. Both of them liked their home comforts and were big foodies.

Rosie couldn't have had a better mentor. I still worried about Lindy. I fretted that her haemolytic anaemia or her cancer might recur but neither disease had showed itself, although she did give us one or two more health scares. In late 2008 she went off her food again and she would, on occasion, become quite distressed, licking the ground and eating grass. She also had terrible wind.

We consulted a homeopathic vet who diagnosed a digestive problem. She suspected Lindy might be intolerant to cereal and advised us to switch to a dog food which didn't contain it. I did as she said and to my great relief Lindy improved immediately. But in the back of my mind there was a niggling doubt that we might not have her for too much longer.

She was quite grey around the muzzle now and I had a feeling that because she'd had such a bad start in life and because she'd had such major health problems she might not live to be a very old dog.

This might sound a bit negative, but actually this knowledge made me focus on making the best of our time together. Lindy might have slowed down, but she still loved her walks and she loved her home comforts.

Lindy had always loved sunshine, which wasn't surprising, given her background. When we'd moved house in 2005 we'd inadvertently picked the hottest day of the year.

Because of this we couldn't leave the dogs in a car as we packed up the removal lorries with our belongings, and we couldn't leave them in the house as the doors were all open. We had tied Abel and Jess up on the decking, which was quite sheltered with a bowl of water, but Lindy soon got fed up of the hard decking and she slipped her collar.

We found her curled up in the front of one of our friend's cars. He had left the driver's door open. It must have been at least thirty degrees centigrade in there but Lindy was in her element. When I tried to move her, she grunted and gave me a quick burst of wriggle-piggle, as if to say, *'I'm perfectly happy where I am, thank you.'*

I couldn't believe she was comfortable in that heat, (most dogs would have been cooked) but she was. I left her to snooze and made sure our friend didn't shut the door.

Anyway, in summer she would find a patch of sunshine and bask in it, and in winter she liked nothing more than to curl up beneath a heater – or if we'd let her she'd curl in her basket right beside the open fire in our lounge. I was a little wary of the latter as I was convinced she'd get burnt by the odd flying sparks but this never happened.

As 2009 wore on, and we had many a long walk in the sunshine, I began to relax. Maybe I was wrong about Lindy. Maybe she would live another few years. Maybe she would become a grand old lady, after all, like Jess had done. All seemed fine.

And then one Friday morning, it was actually the 2nd October, and the date is burned on my mind for various reasons, disaster struck.

We got up early as usual – I was teaching a writing class that day – but I was actually in the shower when Tony called up the stairs, 'Quick, love, there's something wrong with Lindy.'

I raced downstairs. She had been sick in her basket and I saw at once that she couldn't get up. She was panting hard. I had the impression that she'd only just been sick. It looked as though she'd had some sort of seizure, like Abel. It was obviously very serious.

While Tony wrapped her in a blanket and carried her to the car I phoned the vet to tell her we were on our way there.

'Phone me when you get there,' I said to Tony. 'If they say she isn't going to make it I will cancel my class of students and I will come straight over.'

I would have gone with him but that would have

meant leaving a whole class of people wondering why I hadn't turned up.

On the way to class my heart was on overdrive. Please let her be OK, I prayed. Please don't let it be today.

And it seemed my prayers were answered because when Tony phoned he sounded quite upbeat.

'She isn't going to die. She is very ill, but it isn't the haemolytic anaemia. She's on a drip and is stable. We can phone again later for an update.'

This was great news. After I'd finished teaching I raced home and phoned the vet for an update.

'She is very ill,' the vet reiterated, 'but she does seem to be responding to treatment.'

As soon as I put the phone down it rang again. This time it was my mum phoning from Tenerife where she lived for part of the year. 'I don't want to worry you, but your gran has had a fall. I think she's all right, but I'm just letting you know.'

I thanked her and we carried on chatting. We'd both been a bit worried about Gran lately. At ninety-six she still lived on her own but she was getting decidedly frailer. I'd been doing her shopping and popping in as often as I could to keep an eye on her but I didn't live close enough to go every day.

I told Mum about Lindy and also said I'd ring Gran when I put the phone down.

But before I had the chance it rang again. This time it was Gran's cleaner sounding very distressed because she thought Gran should go to hospital as she'd hurt her leg and was bleeding.

'I'm on my way,' I told her and left the house immediately.

Gran lived in a flat but fortunately the communal front door was open and so was her front door. I wasn't prepared for the sight that met me when I went inside. Gran's white hall carpet was covered in bloody footprints. I followed them to the lounge and found Gran walking around and giggling slightly hysterically.

'What on earth have you done?' I gasped.

'I'm fine,' she said. 'Nothing wrong with me.'

This was patently not true, although I still couldn't see where the blood was coming from.

'Please, Gran, just show me where you've hurt yourself,' I begged, and reluctantly she agreed and pulled up the leg of her tracksuit bottom.

She had what I can only describe as a balloon shaped bag of blood attached to her calf. She had wrapped a tea towel around it, and this was blood soaked, and every time she moved more blood spurted from the bag, which I realised had formed from her own stretched skin.

Horrified, I reached for the phone.

'What are you doing?' she yelped.

'Phoning an ambulance,' I said. 'You need to go

to hospital.'

She protested vehemently and was still protesting when the paramedics arrived. But they were wonderful and they very gently managed to persuade her that hospital was the best place for her to be.

I followed in my car. My worries about Lindy had been pushed to the back of my mind but they were still there. At the hospital Gran was taken to a side ward where there was a long wait to see the doctor. It was now around 3 p.m.

At 7 p.m. although Gran had seen a registrar and had a temporary dressing put on her leg, we were still waiting to see someone who would make the decision whether or not to keep her in hospital. I was anxious that she stayed in hospital. I didn't want her going back to her flat alone – not least because it looked like a crime scene and I wanted to get the carpets cleaned before she went home. Gran refused point blank to come back to our house, which she said was cold, and I was also worried about her mental state.

She was usually so sharp, but she seemed muddled and confused. In between waiting for the doctor I'd been nipping outside to phone the vet's for progress reports of Lindy.

The news wasn't good but it wasn't too bad either. She was responding to treatment, she was sitting up, they hadn't worked out what was wrong with her, but they thought she was improving.

At 9 p.m. Gran finally saw a doctor who said, to my great relief, that she must stay in hospital while they sorted out her leg. I phoned to tell Tony that I'd be leaving shortly and asked him to phone the vet for another progress report as my battery was getting low and I didn't want my mobile to conk out midway through a conversation.

Then I finally left the hospital. I was driving through Kinson, which was about halfway home when my phone rang again. It was Tony.

'I'm really sorry,' he began, 'But I just phoned the vet and Lindy passed away an hour ago.'

I remember shouting at him that this couldn't be right. She'd been improving the last time I'd phoned. Poor Tony must have been deafened by my howls of grief. I couldn't see straight for tears. I could certainly no longer drive. I pulled over to the side of the road and I rested my head on the steering wheel and just cried and cried. I thought my heart would break.

Lindy and I had been through so much and I hadn't even had the chance to say goodbye.

Afterword

THERE IS NO HAPPY ending when you lose someone you love. I know from experience that it's as heartbreaking to lose a dog you love as it is to lose a person. This is a truth that has never really surprised me. After all, love is love, and is not determined by whether a creature has two legs or four.

I never planned to get involved with Lindy. I never planned to bring a little stray dog back to England. If I hadn't had such long arms maybe none of it would have happened. But I do know that I feel blessed.

We had her for eight fantastic years. She brought immense joy into our lives. She brought us worries too, but, then, the two usually come hand in hand, don't they? Life was certainly never dull with Lindy around. She lived every one of her nine lives to the full.

She even trained up her successor – Rosie never did get a home – and she has very big paw prints to fill, but I think Lindy would have approved of our decision to keep her. In fact whenever I think about Lindy and her life with us, I smile. Could she have left us a better legacy than that? I don't think so!

Useful Addresses

Dog's Trust
Head Office
Dogs Trust, 17 Wakley Street, London, EC1V 7RQ
www.dogstrust.org.uk

The Society for Companion Animal Studies
(SCAS)
Support for bereaved pet owners
Contact **0800 096 6606** (some mobile networks
may charge) from 8:30am - 8:30pm, or email
pbssmail@bluecross.org.uk.

Useful websites

Dorset Animal Workers Group (DAWG) (Dog
Rescue)
www.dawgdogs.net

Lyn at Happy Dogs (Dog Rescue)
www.happydogsrescue.co.uk

Liz at Somerset and Dorset Animal Rescue
(Animal Rescue)
www.somersetanddorsetanimalrescue.co.uk

Happy Landings (Animal Rescue)
www.happy-landings.org.uk

Jo at Tricks4Treats (Dog Training in Dorset)
www.tricks4treats.co.uk

Also by Della Galton

HELTER SKELTER

Brought up on a seaside fairground, Vanessa knows all about what a rollercoaster ride life can be. Tragedy forces her to flee but when she discovers that her husband, a property developer, is cheating on her she returns. But the fair has gone, the land, bought by her husband, is now covered by luxury flats.

Going back can be painful but this is just the start of the Helter Skelter for Vanessa. While she feels her life is spiralling ever downwards, there are the strong arms of a passion from her past to catch her at the end.

ISBN 9781905170975 Price £6.99

PASSING SHADOWS

How do you choose between friendship and love?
Maggie faces an impossible dilemma when she
discovers that Finn, the man she loves, is also the
father of her best friend's child. Should Maggie
betray her best friend, who never wanted him to
know? Or lie to Finn, the first man she's ever
trusted enough to love? The decision is
complicated by the shadows of her past.

ISBN 9781905170234 Price £6.99

Also from Accent Press

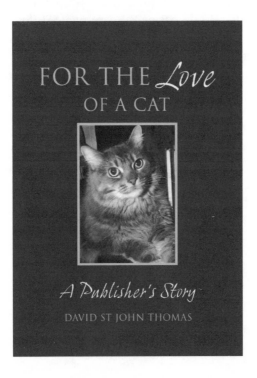

Few people can appreciate the joy that being owned by a cat brings better than David St John Thomas – the latest in a long line of publishers and authors to pay homage to the very special cats who have entered their busy lives. This is a book for everyone who really cares about cats. Vividly written, sometimes serious, sometimes light-hearted, anyone who has fallen for a cat, however much against their better judgement, is bound to find it uplifting. While cat people are nice (Hitler couldn't stand them!), the real heroes in this book are naturally the cats themselves. A rich portfolio of feline characters – including the author's own cats – step off the page, or perhaps lie curled in seductive curves on it, so vividly that you can feel their fur and hear their purr! Rich in entertaining anecdotes and asides, *For the Love of a Cat* will enhance all cat owners' understanding of their feline friend and remind them again and again just how lucky they are to share their lives with this most fascinating of creatures.

ISBN 9781921497360 – £9.99